LITTLE BY LITTLE,
THE BIRD BUILDS ITS NEST

(Petit à petit, l'oiseau fait son nid)

Poems About Birds

Little by Little, The Bird Builds Its Nest

(Petit à petit, l'oiseau fait son nid)

Poems About Birds

Edited by jd hegarty

PARIS MORNING
PUBLICATIONS

Published in 2024 by Paris Morning Publications

www.parismorningpublications.com
Copyright © Paris Morning Publications

Published and reprinted in the United States of America
ISBN: 979-8-218-47743-1
Cover design by Audrey Campbell
Book design and typesetting by Mayfly book design

When I was a junior high student, I began studying French. My teacher's name was Sister Peronne Marie, an elegant and gentle – if not occasionally stern – nun. I loved the fact that I was somehow, at age 13, sophisticated enough to learn French but at the same time, it didn't exactly come naturally to me.

One of the phrases from those early years of my studies that I've never forgotten is the title of this anthology – and when I think of it, it always echoes in my mind in French and not in English: petit à petit, l'oiseau fait son nid.

It's a lovely expression and a true one. Everything in this life is "petit à petit" or "little by little." It's rare that anything we do is successful on the first try. We have to find the spot, gather the sticks, see what works and what doesn't work, until we have created whatever nest we intend to build. In our lifetimes, we will build many nests.

The poems in this collection celebrate birds of all kinds – beautiful songbirds, homely stalwarts – and eloquently describe the work they do to find their place in the natural world. We observe their persistence, their glory, their stillness, their noise.

Little by little - petit à petit – these poems invite us to build our own "nests" of appreciation for the world that surrounds us.

Julie Pfitzinger
Publisher

HATCH

EGG

MaryAnn Franta Moenck

This dream has no wings —

Keep it warm.

CROWS

Carol Rucks

Once, crows were my best friends.
I used to watch them strut beneath the pine trees,
showing their backsides to each other.
No one seemed to notice that I was in their company.
Today I saw an old friend. Her black hair shimmered
like the sun-touched head of a god.
On seeing me, she turned her gaze away
to look into the green space just ahead.
My heart thumped, remembering a lie I told her
while urging thunder out of a silent sky.

QUESTIONS FOR THE MOUNTAIN BLUEBIRD

Michael S. Moos

You might ask the mountain bluebird what is the secret
of his happiness. Ask how he came to love the work he is given.
There will be a pause, of course, as he looks into your eyes,
searching for any trace of the wild you might still carry.
There must have been a time when we did not need words.
A way of reading the wind
and the trail leading off through the tall grasses.
Sometimes you want to peel back your skin,
find the other one you were, before the mechanisms of desire
became coded in your cells.
Do you wonder how pain began?
Not the grounding by wounds, but the other, deeper pain,
sibling of loneliness, that completes you.
If you do not see how the doe grieves over her new fawn torn
by coyotes in the early morning light, you are lost.
If you cannot feel how we are all connected, we are lost.
This much seems clear.
If you are torn open by the certainty of having to leave this place
you have come to love, you are alive enough.
Being broken open is a gift. If you are willing.
What else do you need to know?

BATH TIME FOR THE ROBINS, ST. LUKE'S DAY, OCTOBER 18

Patrick Hansel

The mid-afternoon sun quivers
out from behind its clouds and
finds the shades of green
that had been sleeping
among the brown and golden fleece
of the streamside marsh. Chickadees
buzz in with their chip-chip-chip,
and on the shag bark oak the downy
woodpecker begins its search
for a tea-time feast. Blue jays
preen and snap, golden finches flit,

and in the slow bend of the stream,
one by one the robins fluff and flap
their wings in the shallows, splashing
water on their gingered breasts.
Only the males are left—their mates
have flown to Mexico and further
south—and so the pumpkin-chested
males, proud as hunters in
their vests, practice the age-old
healing proverb: after godliness,
cleanliness is best.

ALL WINGED CREATURES

Timothy Young

An oriole sings from the cedar's top,
"I am a bright bird!"
and a brown bat drops like a wasp
from the garage's eave
to feed in the maple grove.

Overhead, that high satellite in orbit
won't reflect the sun for long,
although fireflies will flicker
all night in the yard.

I was told that all winged creatures
see into the spiritual world,
and half the time they see into ours.
I know I'll never see enough
of this lovely, living world.

For a few hours the bat
will see what I can't,
and the oriole will watch over
its hanging pouch of eggs.
Dawn will come, and the bird will see it
long before I do or am able.

THE BIRDS KNOW IT

Tim Nolan

That's what I hear from the next booth
From the old couple younger than me

Who just came off the golf course what
Do the birds know that's what I want to

Know other than their song for a definite
Time and place I don't think they were

Talking about bird songs they meant
Something else and now they're talking

About little things around the house water
The geraniums put every dish in the house

Into the dishwasher so all are done at once
And about absolutely nothing more it's

Amazing how much can be said about so
Little I guess the birds do know it for sure

MORNING

Jaqi Holland

At roofline, eyeline,
a mourning dove
fills its thin bill with water
from the gutter,
tucking beak into body,
fluffing feathers
to lift the night's slumber.

I splash water on my face
from the basin,
drink a glass, awaken,
this morning like the last.

Does the dove contemplate
routine—cleaning, preening
roosting, feeding—stunned
at another dull morning,
or is every moment not
in a talon's grip a gift,
some benevolent god of prey
sparing the small
lives of birds?
Might I pray to that god, too?

DUCK EGGS

Jim Lenfestey

I'm told the duck agreed to this,
her children held up to the light, half-
a-dozen translucent orbs rising from
sunlit grass.

We crack each opal open slowly,
sunset sliding down the shell's horizon
to butter's bubbly ocean.

Breakfast of light,
measure of our days,
purloined from the holy altar
of a golden nest,

I hatch you
into strength I did not feel,
dreams I did not know,
hope I did not have.

I begin my day with a nasal honk
from my monstrous beak, the leading edge
of a now most purposeful waddle.

LETTER TO EDWIN WAY TEALE
FROM THE HUDSON VALLEY, 2022

Alison Granucci

Dear Edwin (if I may),

You never knew me but I grew up with you. Your curious title
North with the Spring chirped like a bird to me on my parents'
bookshelf, so every April when my family trekked two days
home from my grandfather's North Carolina farm—southern
blooms at their *exuberant peak*—I watched from the backseat,
silently *kept pace with the unfolding bud and expanding leaf.*
If the lavender blossomed tree was a jacaranda, redbud, or
weeping cherry, I'll never know, but lonely in the expanse of
station wagon, I headed north in secret affinity with you.

Like *homegoing warblers*, our annual migration had us back
for a second Spring, Connecticut blossoms opening anew
in concert with the waking of *earthworms and robin*—precisely
when the thermostat rises to a given point. Today our earth
is heating up. The climate is migrating, awry. The *first greening
leaf* emerges too soon, *the endlessly meshing gears of nature's
machine* are ensnarled.

Edwin, when your son was killed in World War II, you shared
with us how you and Nellie traversed the wilds of your grief
by immersing yourselves in the expanse of Nature. Tell me,
how then do we grieve the loss of Nature herself? Were you
still with us, I like to think your next book would issue forth
the *wild, far-carrying wail* of the river limpkin—your voice
lifted into *a caterwauling crescendo* echoing back to us
a sharp loneliness from the false Spring of shifting seasons.

Instead, I hear the long ago chirp of *North with the Spring*—
the same old copy tucked now on my shelf—I dust its torn cover,
read it at last. Edwin, more than forty Octobers have passed since
you *curved into the wind* on your final *vertical migration*—I love
to imagine what daring *aerial trails* you carved through that
bird-swept mist before you were too-soon met on the other side
by the last Bachman's warbler. But through such mists your words
make the trek, the way *crows come back*, and barn swallows,
home from Brazil; like yellow warblers winging in from Yucatan,
and bobolinks, from Argentina, flying north.

With love, always,
Alison

SPARROWS

Rob Hardy

The prairie looks bigger than it is
because of the sky.

It takes a while to orient myself
to the sparrow
singing on the dry stalk of compass plant.

These birds have a funny way of vanishing
as soon as I spot them,
ventriloquists giving their voices to the grass.

I could devote my life to sparrows.
I could spend the rest of my days
separating brown of bird
from brown of grass,
learning sparrow as a second language.

Song.
Savannah.
Chipping.
Henslow's.

What a luxury it is
to live among ordinary things!

I would become endemic,
belonging only to this place,
my entire life contained
in these 800 hectares of tall grass.

I'm nearing sixty—
about time to sail off into eccentricity,
childhood's opposite shore.

The best days will be
the days when I'm caught in the rain.

SONG FOR DOGEN

(for katagiri roshi)
Dougie Padilla

lanky blue heron stands in shallow water
maybe 50 feet from where i sit
on my park bench doing shikantaza.

he rarely moves.

when he does, it's only a gawky step or two
and then he's impeccably still again.

suddenly, in a flash,
his long beak hits the water,
snatches a small silver fish,
and quickly gulps it down
his long skinny throat
to a waiting belly

and, then, simply,
he returns

to standing

still.

THE WOULD-BE NATURALIST GOES BIRDING

D.E. Green

So those four eagles I saw yesterday—
they turned out to be turkey vultures,
circling low over the pond and the field,
tilting and shimmying on a brisk wind.

It felt a little like the loss of patriotism
back when I was in college and Nixon
fired Archibald Cox and proved he was
the presidential liar I'd denied he was.

Mistaking those vultures for eagles—losing
those damned eagles—felt like losing faith
in the one holy, catholic, and apostolic
church. All over again. Wasn't once enough?

So this morning I went out with an urbane
biologist who admitted he wasn't sure either
about the bird that swooped down over us,
scavenging, its eye peeled for something

to fill its maw, like Nixon, not trusting
the democracy he believed he was defending
to give him the votes he needed, and so grabbing
them instead. Nature's hunger, American greed—

you understand better, after eagles disappear,
turn vulture, that we live among the dead,
that large black wings cast shadows over us—
harbingers of grief, those night-dark silhouettes.

THE BIRDS OF PARADISE

Mike Hazard

Weird: weird birds are everywhere. Birds with no names known
to this bird-brained egghead who gets by, by faking bird calls.
One bird I don't know the name of seems to be asking me a
    question.
I imitate it—back and forth, like electricity we buzz and pause,
when so clear an eye cocks at me—I fancy I see an owl of
    Shangrila,
a cardinal of Eden, a canary of Nirvana, and a crow of Utopia.
A bluebird of happiness perches on the crown of the blue star
    kachina!
In a flight of free fancy, I glide like a ring-necked pheasant.
I stick my neck out like a trumpeter swan. I keen like an eagle.
I flock with all the birds of this whole, flocking world...
I fancy we want to look and see, right into each other's eyes,
and learn by heart all the sacred songs of the birds of paradise.

HERMIT THRUSH

Zorzalito Colirrufo
Grive Solitaire
Diane Jarvenpa

Not lost, not found,
the ground's rough bristle
seals me in
a common precinct.

Tunes thread in patchy light,
rare goods on forest floor.
Try to find the right one
and that is about

how wind fills lungs
and how the belly burns
with the unknown.
I sing to the understory,

to bloodroot and gooseberry,
into dark shadows of trees.
How they sometimes answer,
their branches shedding error

or defeat endured in the day.
Their unburdened shadow
meeting my shadow, maybe
some day meeting yours.

BIRD, OR WHAT COULD BECOME ONE

Julia Klatt Singer

There is no warning
When the sky asks you
To pick up one of its pieces.

At first you don't even recognize
What it is, naked as an alien
Too small to be threatening

You notice it is breathing.
Eyes blank spots, shaped
like saucers, skin transparent

Something in you
opens; you think water
You think worm.

You think like a mother.
Check the wet ground.
Turn stones.

You've never been so

Delighted to see a slug.
Bird. Or what will become

one. You recognize
The mouth unhinged.
You recognize the hunger.

MORNING, AT THE BROWN BRINK EASTWARD

Sabrina Kirby

Kwan Yin in my window, her back to the sun, appears
to be missing an arm. But the arm is there, its hand the very one
that cups the healing vessel as She Who Hears the Cries of the World
stands by, this Easter morning, while bicyclists circle the quad,
the usual Sunday campus silence punctuated by whirrs
of spoked wheels and sprockets, by echo-muffled shouts
and whoops urging the racers on.

Just as still, just as alert, just as silent sits the dove
in the spruce by my front door, her loose nest of twigs
held together as much by her weight from above
as by branches spread like a thumb and two fingers below.
Papa dove must feed her, for she never seems to move
except to rotate through the compass points, morning
through afternoon, evening into night. Like the ceramic
goddess, mama dove broods in deep reserve, immanent
yet remote: she is here, she is not risen. Jostle her or
make her fly, she goes nowhere, she endlessly returns.

THE YOUNG BIRDWATCHER

Jim Rogers

When May got most ripe
we visited Acacia Park.
Grandma hauled a tub
of lilacs on her hip

cut to dress Preston's
and Granny Wigginton's graves
and that of Evans Rogers,
dead since 1936.

Adults looked after flowers
while we roamed about,
understanding not to run
down cemetery hills, or shout.

Women who knew the dead
kept their calendar;
I kept my own.
Each year this visit meant

I'd spot gold- and ruby-
crowned kinglets –
almost the smallest of birds,
hardly bigger than moths --

stopped on their flight
north, in the windbreak
row of spruces
near my uncle's grave.

They would flit in and out
while the women brushed away
matted grass, fussed,
and then stood silent,

as I imagined deep Canada
where kinglets nest:
an endless pine-blue forest
filled with such birds,

the cold upper reach
of a continent
in which even the treetops
know only shade.

FLIGHT

PTARMIGAN! PTARMIGAN!

Alamgir Hashmi

I last saw it preening as a blueberry
patch some other place, and gosh,
here it is now, this one,
amid trees of heaven,

riotous red hemlock, larch and fir.
Whisper spruce, and with hisses,
low whistles and clucks, the leaves
stir uneasy, so I can tell the feather,

chest spot, or band from the rest.
Foraging far in the pine country—
needles after green shoots—it has altered
again, melting into the landscape;

shelters easy with flamboyant sumac,
letting in the fast underbrush, loud spice.
Lush mountainside, seeds, berries, lake
waters fill this dusky hornbeak

no matter the brownish desert kin
daily bathes in the dust. And in the park today,
looking up into treetops, I may have
overstepped the peace, tubers

or dry branches crackling everywhere.
So it looks out of red eyes, sore—
sideways of its nervous coat
of shifting colors,

scampers on the touchy ground,
wings spread out once, twice, clapped shut,
and readies to take the forest along
crazy brusque in flight.

FLYING COLORS

Mike Hazard

While my birding buddies look aloft
in the budding branches and blue skies,
listening for songs of a feather,
I linger among the long green grasses
loaded with dew drops, chanting silently
"debauchee of dew, debauchee of dew."
Zooming in closer I realize,
at a thousand points of view,
with tiny motions of my eyes,
each bead of water shoots a new
firework of colored light,
a mirror of birds in flight:
red cardinal, orange oriole,
yellow flicker, green heron,
blue-winged warbler, indigo bunting,
purple martin.

We pause with our binoculars,
mesmerized as we try to memorize
the tiny song of a sparrow
we cannot see or name for sure:
Baird's? grasshopper? Henslow's?
Somewhere over the rainbows
a song of a tiny sparrow
calls us across the meadow.

I WILL BE GONE

Dougie Padilla

and one day my mother let our yellow canary out to clean the
    birdcage and someone had
left the window open somewhere in the house and boom our
    canary was gone, gone out
that window, gone from the neighborhood, gone from the
    planet soon most likely.

someimes, i feel like that canary, that it will come my time, and
    i'll sprint for an open
window, then i'll take off and follow my instincts to the next
    world. and those i love and
that love me will be frantic, will search for me everywhere. but i
    will be everywhere and
nowhere. and i will be gone.

i will be gone.

GREAT HORNED OWL AND THE STARS

Michael Kiesow Moore

Owl takes flight,
home in the crepuscular sky.
Yellow orbs
shine like two bright moons.
Her wings rewrite celestial navigation.

CEDAR WAXWINGS

Thomas R. Smith

The other day I thought, Summer's
almost over and I still haven't seen
any waxwings. Now I'm standing at
one of my favorite spots on the river
shore and here they are, grinning
their joy through their little black
bandit masks, flitting and cavorting
in their clowning manner. Always in groups,
always keeping up their aerobatics
as if for nothing more than the joy of it,
looping and diving among the willows
overhanging the water, never staying
in one place long. Sometimes the crests
standing up on their buffy heads
seem to shiver in wild delight,
one of those worlds Blake saw closed
by our "senses five." Grateful
to have found them again, I open wide
my healing heart's sky to let in
their crazybird air show medicine.

I WATCH THE BIRDS IN THEIR CHAOTIC

Jessica Simmons

pattern, flying above ice-
covered streets. What halts us
has no sway over them; if anything,
the cold seems to invigorate their flight. Wings slash
through each frozen bullet
raining towards a world they don't walk
on-it melts against their feathers as they fly
faster-I am certain nothing can stop them.

SWAN SONGS

Timothy Young

Great hollers fall from the sky.
At two hundred and twelve
I lose count of the tundra swans in one vee.
Like a long raft riding the wind
they fly toward the sun
as it slips blushingly,
in and out of a purple cloud,
above blue bluffs and reflects
on the silver sheen of the river.

More than three thousand swans
have passed overhead in the last hour,
and they're still coming and going.
There's a fire in my chest.
More singing begins in the southeast.
Approaching....'proaching....'proaching.

I am so excited.
I may never witness this again,
but, I need and want to go
to Jesse's last high school concert
where he will play his clarinet solo
in that old song of longing,
Oh, Shenandoah.

CROWS IN EARLY WINTER

(Near Black River Falls)
Jim Rogers

Pulling away from the roadside rest,
and the bronzed account of passenger pigeons
netted by the clumsy million
in just these woods,
I enter the flow of traffic
streaming south, carried along
like a twig tossed onto a current.

Crows pass overhead, indifferent to me,
to the road, to the story of the pigeons.
They are weaving their own net,
it seems, headed this way or that
with an intent of their own.

I think I know what the crows know:
the land will belong to them:
The halted fields,
the absurd billboards urging us
to some estival foolishness, the brown
stubble; the snow growing
icy in the winter sun.

A slow storytelling of crows in the air
reclaims this leftover land.

SPRING FLOOD

Donna Isaac

On a road trip out west, we grew weary of the high turns,
endless sky. A sign read, "See the Bear," but we never did.

Not until an osprey snatched a fish from a swollen stream,
a good omen, did our spirits rise and open our eyes:

- A snorting herd of buffalo, five calves in tow, forded the
  Firehole River.
- A harem of wild horses uprooted and smunched grass off
  Highway 89.
- A moose amid paintbrush and glacier lilies bit off a dry twig.
- Three mountain goats sported beards like icicles, clumps of
  winter coats.

At dusk, I faced west, tobacco in hand,
praised the Blackfeet, the huckleberries, the day.

A flickertail flew up out of the grass,
and the sun, a pearl upon a satin sky, sank.

These were the gifts foretold by the osprey,
secrets of the sage-green waters rushing by.

SNOWY EGRET

Michael S. Moos

In the dusk the wings of a snowy egret open, to carry
the plump body back along the rocky shore, toward the bones
of the rookery, patiently, silently, slowly.
As your body sometimes carries your heart patiently, slowly,
silently toward conciliation, a door leading into clear air.
Leading you into the chambers made up of uncertain reflections,
shadows passing over the ground. Not knowing why.
A music never written out, only heard and carried
from one time to another, with all those fragile hopes
rising up like white birds out of the bare trees of memory,
where charred timbers linger in the cool prairie wind,
and the river continues to move with its tireless wisdom
between the silent tigerlilies, growing wild
under the lasting blue skies you remember from childhood,
waking on summer mornings to the voices of mourning doves
calling to something faint, not yet lost.

CROW

Scott Vetsch

A solitary crow draws itself across
the bleak winter sunset.

A coarse flapping calligraphy
above the leafless oaks.

Sky frozen and wide,
crow homeless and free.

OWLS

Becky Boling

I

The owls were out
in the tree yesterday.
People milled around,
tugged on recalcitrant dogs,
herded flocks of children.

Heads turned at uncomfortable
angles, knees and feet
wobbled for purchase.
We stared through leaves,
infused life into crisscrossed
limbs and gnarled wood
until at last we honed in
on the objects of our gaze.

Above us,
wings flexed,
heads swiveled,
cautious inhuman eyes
stared down at us.

Predators, aren't we all?
Why do we stand, transfixed?
Risk vertigo? Swaying
branches rock us on our heels.
To catch a glimpse
of a raptor and its young?

What drama is this that does
not so much unfold as stop
time in freeze frames,
leaving us to spin on our axis—
vibrations on a taut wire?

We long to transgress
the urban landscape,
escape the squared
corners of our edifices,
the flat pavement of our roads.

II

On greened branches
downy-backed owlets
test claws, practice
silence and stealth
in plain view.

The show begins,
audience rapt, necks craned.

From their wooden hollow,
peer fuzzy-winged raptors.
We hold our breath.
I-phones digitalize,
post and share,
frame by frame,
their frozen stare.

Flotsam caught in the eddy
of a stream, couples, families,

lone walkers, eyes tangled
in the canopy, anticipate the scene.
Some drift off, others arrive,
search for the best angle.
Clustered beneath the boughs,
we whisper, testify, conjecture,
bit players awaiting our cue.

An adult owl hovers
several trees distant,
emits a deep throaty call
a febrile, high double-time note,
an invisible tether flung
over our pivoting heads
to the nest above.

III

Where?
Fingers point.
Eyes strain.
Each visit requires
a new orientation.
We share the role of guide,
inheriting knowledge,
passing it on.

There. Alone the owlets,
less fuzz, more wing,
move about in patterns
up, down, across.
No one stands guard,

except those of us
who come each day,
to mark their change.

Soon, we say, we'll come
to find them gone.

BETWEEN BURSTS OF THUNDER, WE HEAR THE ROBINS

Greg Watson

If we cannot learn the song
of these birds, calling through
the shuddering dark, let us at least
learn their silence.

If we cannot know the secrets
of their flight, let us at least
acquire the stillness they have
perfected on thin air.

VIEWS OF A PEACOCK

New Ulm, Minnesota
Steven McCown

Above us,
atop a Victorian mansion,
his emerald blue "eyes "opening
wider and wider open our eyes
as if we tourists on the ground
have never seen a world in a pair of wings—
bright whorls, starry night
in the afternoon.

He descends,
flying over a deer park,
gazebos and a brick-path flower
garden— a floating tapestry alighting
upon a stack of palettes outside
Schell's Brewery.

A visionary
on a roughhewn stage,
he extends wings as if to embrace
barrels of beer, forklifts sputtering past,
men and women at work,
the world as he sees it
and as it is.

UNTIL I SEE YOU AGAIN

Julia Klatt Singer

The morning you left
Smelled of elderflowers and rain.

It will take a hard rain
To wash your scent
From my body.

All day, the moon is a ghost
on my right shoulder.

How can something so light
Fill me.

I am learning Jay and Sparrow and Crow.
And yes, it is mostly about longing;
where and for whom.

Six blue jays wing into the yard, alight
And like my thoughts, fly to you.

Do you think of me? Does the sway of a branch,
The curve of a stone having you wondering

Where I am, what is in my hands.

I tally the times I want for you
Until I too have a forest.

The quickest way to you:
This energy, this air.

This is how you find me, waiting
For you, for you

To fly, your way, to me.

CANADA GEESE ON THE HIGHWAY

Tim Nolan

They are dumb no question
Not crows who can count

Have some self-awareness
Still Canada Geese fly south

In neat formation honk to
One another a beautiful ease

They have you can distinctly
Hear their wings overhead

Their honking so close it might
Be your own honking so close

On the highway they walk in dazed
Circles can't even decide to cross

Dumb Fucking Birds—yet I slammed
To a stop—because I know they can fly

MY BROTHERS

Rebecca Paradis

The morning air carries
A choral cooing and hooting from up the bluff,
Not the neighbor's children,
Nor the garish gobble of wild turkeys,
Not the eerie choir of coyotes,
Nor the brass honk of Canada geese,
Under the silver cloud cover
A surge of swans
Glinting bright white
Appears over me,
A choreographed chorus, they curve
Back over my treetops toward
The lap of the lake in the cemetery,
That instant
Before turning,
They are my enchanted brothers
And I hold up twelve nettle shirts
Stitched in silence over six long years.
The swans land all around me
And rescue me
From a witch's burning,
As I rescue them
From the sky.

REVENGE OF THE PSEUDO-RAVENS. 2021

Patrick Hansel

A few blocks from the George Floyd
Memorial lies the brick and mortar word-store
Called Hosmer Library. The last of four
libraries Carnegie built in the city. You can
only "grab and go" these masked days,
no lingering over magazines, and only
children can use computers, for homework only.

Driving down 4th Avenue, I interrupt
a small scale murder: eleven crows feasting
on a dead cat in the middle of the road.
They pick at the carcass in a secret order:
no one goes hungry, no one is pushed out
of the circle for what they have done or not

done. This feast is for all. I am almost
upon them before they rise, eleven black
seraphs, wings slapping the low winter sun
as they scatter. Their departing leaves
a wound on the ground: red meat almost
pulsing, grey fur bereft. The grateful

crows, who mate for life, who raise offspring
not their own and can make tools to make
other tools, swiftly return to the banqueting
table as I pass, no pushing or shoving, no
chattered warnings. I walk down the street
with the two volumes of MN history I am

returning: page upon page of governors
and titans, all come from Europe, now

enshrined in the names of streets and counties
and schools across the state. The crowd
of winged diners do not complain about me
breaking up the feast. They continue their
reclamation in peace. Paw, catgut, stolen
eye will grow into their wings. Meat to meat,
flesh to flesh, a bird eater eaten in peace.

PERCH

WINDOW KILLS

(for Joan Cox)
Jim Rogers

After we had gone through the closet, winnowing
all but the finest of clothes (suitable to be buried in,
was our unspoken thought), and allowed the bills
to arrive in a bolus at month's end until unforeseen
debts could no longer slap us in the face; after
we had pieced together an address book of sorts
out of old envelopes and paper scraps tucked in the desk,
after we'd come to believe we had tidied up
our mother's life, we opened the freezer.

In the frosty dark we found a dozen or more bird
cadavers, songbirds that had dropped x number of stories
to the street, only feathers to cushion their crash landing.
When Icarus fell there was at least a sense that balance
had been restored, hubris given its due comeuppance.
Not so these fallen creatures. The worst this Purple Finch
had done was mistake its reflection for another bird,
and lost that game of flinch. Hardly a capital offense,
to be misled, but office towers scarcely care.

But she did. Taxidermy may be a feeble hope
yet it was the hope she held. We thought of her lifting
a lifeless bird off the sidewalk, carrying it home in her purse
with her lipstick, her compact, her keys. The poet
was right: Hope *is* the thing with feathers.
She kept her wished-for restoration frozen,
stacked like ears of sweetcorn. Kept a rock-hard

fire-orange oriole. Kept woodpeckers that once could drill
their way through hundred-year oak, found dead
after one sick thud. Kept a bead-emerald hummingbird
that now looked like a sausage encrusted with freezer burn.
And a Redstart that must have been skipping through air
one crystal morning when it simply, suddenly, stopped.

TWENTY DRUNKEN ROBINS

(Anderson Center, Sunday morning, 7 October)
Jim Lenfestey

This I have never seen before:
a flock of twenty drunken robins
like happy children roiling the dusty
quilt of fallen oak leaves in October,
happy and chasing and free
under the flashing sign of a red berry tree.

They are fat, and many, and young ones.
And I must say happy again,
loud songs waking later sleepers,
leaf dancing rustling up a racket,
so many bright berries this year of drought.

As if two leaves suddenly flew up,
two fledglings drunkenly cavort
in the nearby yew, then pause
like eager children in a game of tag,
black eyes glistening, white spectacles
framing an ecstatic look.

They flurry back to the red berry bar,
raising as they alight their charcoal cloaks
trimmed in ermine white
to dazzle me.

What a happy scene, this berry tree
I did not know, but robins do, rising

from tanned leather bur oak leaves
fallen here like paws of bears
thick as a feather mattress where
happy native birds dive in flurries.

My friend tended this berry tree
a decade and a half
for fresh thrush friends
to find and love today,
and drunken, gladden me.

BLUE JAY

Becky Boling

A slice of sky, he
lights on my porch.

Between blue spandrels
and carved peach spindles
framed. A royal profile
from sweeping blue crest
to sleek black beak
he poses, all stillness.

There he perches
as if the trim on my porch
were a tree limb, birch or oak.

Sable stripes on a blue canvas
about the eye, on wing,
distinguish him from sky.

His mate flits by, too quick
for sight, except as shadow
across porch then skyward
beyond my window frame.

Blue jay rests blue on blue
a moment more, then off—
blue into blue.

IT IS IMPORTANT TO ME TO TALK TO BIRDS.

Dougie Padilla

it is important to me to talk to birds.
it is important to me that those birds listen,
that they take the time to sit there
and have a moment
so our friendship can grow.

it is important to me to sit on the deck
and see the elegant future,
what with all its strands racing off ahead,
out beyond the corn and soybeans,
into the woods and ravines
down towards the chippewa.

it is important to me to have grandchildren,
grandchildren that I can touch,
even as they wander the far worlds,
even as they build shacks
made of apples and lilacs.

it is important for me right now,
this very week,
to take a step or two or twenty,
back from the crazy worlds,
the newspaper worlds,
the internet worlds,
the worlds that climb all over each other
strangling life from the dew
the marigolds sleep on.

may those in power
and those out of power
share the beauty of all things,
of all things layered
and endless.

may the birds speak freely
with each and every one of you,
and with each other.
may you listen and respond
in a language you cannot hold
or even dream of.

and may you soar over lake pepin each fall
as you start your everlasting journey southward
for a warmer winter nearer to the sea -
and the lands we all arise from,
the lands we all return to.

BLACK-HEADED GROSSBEAKS

Pheucticus melanocephalus
Amelia Díaz Ettinger

to my surprise as i wonder
about this morning's nature gift,
in Roger Tory Peterson's field guide
the towhee and the grossbeaks
live side by side, frozen in profile.

Grossbeaks seldom visit us
here in these dense fir and larch woods
sunshine reaches slowly as the sun
toils through branches and opens
in the meadow to our south

my myopic eyes awoke to the sight
of a flock of males and a female
swirling in the frenzy of spring desire
right here on this lawn, this privilege
i became a voguer in an avian drama

a spread of feathers and silent competition
the female feeds on bits left over
by the lawnmower—pretending
she does not see the wings spread
for her delight, her rhapsody

ahh, to be that young again

OUTSIDE THE RITE-AID PHARMACY

Dan McGleno

12 minutes before opening
I helped a homeless guy scrounge cigarette butts from the curb
A woman showed up, about Mother's age, wearing a floppy hat
And a pair of binoculars
I asked, if she was going birding
She answered...
Yes, I just came from the water
Ducks are about to start migrating
I asked how it went
She said, Great
How many did you see?
I didn't see any
Instantly, I became confused
She smiled and explained
You have to watch the mornings
They aren't there
If you want to be there
The morning they get there

ODE TO THE FAMILY OF CROW

Jim Lenfestey

I love your language
spoken in the woodlot
behind the house,
clack and purr,
growl and hum and moan.

Behind the window screen
that separates us forever,
you click and coo to babies,
yell to teens, "tell us,
tell us, tell us
where you are."

How smart you are!
You learn our language,
feast at the wheels of our cars,
know when the garbage is out,
know when we sleep,
how angry we are,
if we own guns.

Black as starless night –
not even the blackbird's yellow eye,
the snowy egret's yellow foot –
your slick feathers eat light
like an oil slick eats light.

As a plane falls from the sky,
you fall from the sky, a shroud.
Carrion delight at your arrival,
only the living dart and complain.
Like night, you own half the world.

I have come to love all of you,
rowing your darkness at dusk
in flocks across the winter sky,
roosting as a thriving city in a
neighborhood of barren trees.

BOY AND GULL

D.E. Green

The old man reaches the stream
that marks the northern verge
of his morning walk
along the slate waters
of Lake Michigan's eastern shore.
As he pivots to return,
he puts on his left the sun rising
over the dunes' verdant heights.
He notices the gulls dotting
the stretch of beach ahead,
well above the watermark,
the path of his return.

Just then a boy
hurtles down
the last steps
of the steep descent
through the wooded dune,
arcs across the wide expanse
of hot bright sand
to the water's edge,
then swoops back
toward a lone gull
he must have spied
as he'd descended.

The large gull ruffles its feathers,
hobbles a few unsteady paces
down the beach. But the boy
keeps coming, keeps running
toward the wary bird that—
sensing his proximity and speed—
flaps its wings, rises slightly,
and glides a few yards south.

The boy quickens his pace and runs—
face skyward now, arms outstretched.
The old man quickens too, feels,
for the moment, exuberant and free.

As the boy circles back out of view,
the old man shifts his gaze
to that old gull, returned at last
to the safety of its fellows,
and pecking at something
in the sand.

SPARROWS

Tim Nolan

Just here in the parking lot one
Two three sparrows jumping down

From the crabapple tree five six
I can't count how many going about

Their business joyfully looking for
Something to eat ten or more now

I'm thinking they're from the same
Extended family they seem to know

Each other the way they land near no
Fear just survival that's all that's it

UNTITLED

Barry MacDonald

I saw a pileated woodpecker
gripping cottonwood bark with its talons
with a furious will it set upon
the tree with a pulverizing patter
stabbing with its beak faster and deeper
than one could suppose without looking on
the scarlet crested woodpecker is gone
the cottonwood didn't live much longer
there was a gaping hole left by the bird
every day I watched the tree through seasons
seeing that splendid gnarly tower leaf
in the spring and my admiration stirred
and then the lightning struck without reason
so its gangly existence came to grief.

GEESE MANEUVERS

Thomas R. Smith

At the cross-quarter. Clouds decide how much brightness to allot to earth. Some light manages to straggle through, silver the river on which hundreds of Canada geese gather. Each is a dark Arthurian craft magicked here by the primordial imagination of the universe.

They are in a state of dynamic flow — one moment their slender-prowed silhouettes rest at anchor, then become a field in motion towards a common point. From relative calm an agitation builds, from quiet a surround of voices noisy as a canyon full of barking dogs. All face in the same direction until, given some crucial signal, their clamor reaches a furious pitch and they cyclone upward, tearing off pieces of the river with their wings and feet. Squadrons appear to rehearse their migratory protocols, flock downstream only to circle back again to the settling water. It's a mystery who commands these maneuvers and how others know to join: "I'm ready!" "Me too!" "I'm in!" "Let's go!"

It can be hypnotic, this surging energy, rhythmic as the breathing of an immense lung. We could stand all day and watch their comings and goings, tumultuous departures and returns to the endlessly accommodating river.

BLESSING

Donna Isaac

Cedar waxwings pull red berries,
    flicking rain-freckled foliage
        with wet beaks.

A museum of three
    upon a tree pass and share
        the tiny sphere.

We could learn from and be
    like these black-masked birds
        with lisping cries.

My mother fed the hungry,
    BOGO coupons for extra cans,
        church casseroles.

Our feeder hosts wrens, chickadees,
    a cardinal giving a sunflower
        to his trembling mate awaiting.

Putin terrorizes, takes, and kills
    his people, his neighbors.
        They flee, babes in arms.

    Why are we not like our mothers,
        gentle birds upon a branch?

What have we learned
    from nature, history,
        fragility of life?

THE SMALL DISASTER

Carol Rucks

Rooftop birds
flock to trees,
their sound
is uttered
on the shingles.
They are snails
that crawl across
the telephone wires.
The wall is gray,
it slides against
the black sun.
The wall carries
no birds,
it spoils our
old dreaming
with its
flat wood.
The wall is gray,
it slides against
the black sun.

WE LIVE TO LOVE

Mike Hazard

We live to love days like today.
Blue sky. Gold branches. Red bird.
With a beguiling, bejeweled song
a musical cardinal is calling
you and me from the top of his tree
to come see a pair of love birds
who coo and coo so I hardly notice
their brown bag and holy smoke.
The spring sun blesses everything.
The Mississippi River's flowing.
A bird on the tree of life is singing.
"We live to love days like today.
We live to love days like today."

WESTERN MEADOWLARK

Sturnella neglecta
Amelia Díaz Ettinger

no one does springtime like you
stocky brown with white banners

reminiscent of surrender flags
a ceasefire of your own

though lewis and clark
forgot to mention you, so your name

'neglecta' among Blackbirds and Orioles,
but abandoned you are not

you have the sheen—fêted to be Oregon's bird
like those pursuers, the pioneers

—you look for open wide spaces
grassland to conquer without a pilfer

spring livens with your melodic
watery call, nature's flute

you perch on demarcating fences
puffing your yellow chest

to proudly display your black 'V'
as if etched by a child's marker

what do say as you sing
your double notes?

you are right
to show this pride

GAME AND SUCH

Alamgir Hashmi

It may have been a Monday morning.
My path in the woods
was the clear voice of the quail,
where none was heard before.
There were others of course, playfully
breaking lithe branches from the sheshams
of this unheard-of wood,
whose green fell after.
Someone's faltering step hissed all the way,
so that no bird would slip a feather,
while I had hardly begun to call.
Autumnal, though fresh,
the trails became dense,
rumours patterned the leaf-fringe
with certain blue flowers of fine fascination,
and yellow, pale, famished animals
who ate only blue;
even a cactus there
feigned a flower or two.
I had no one by me
to whisper the anticipation,
to say Yes, now I have seen one,
when I had seen;
but that was just as well.
I took my hand in my own hand
and—waiting for the wind to start—
followed in the way the trees inclined.

GOOD FRIDAY WALK

Rob Hardy

Walking along the path,
through the old field overgrown
with pigeon grass and dry

stalks of sceptered goldenrod,
with each step I raised
an eruption of flickers from the grass,

a flash of yellow underwing,
white rump hoisting its flag of retreat.
I thought each one of them

had to be the last, but still another
and another launched itself
into the arms of the leafless trees.

Finally, I stopped,
with dozens of flickers still
rising from the brown earth all around.

I stood with my arms outstretched,
as if I had opened myself, and released
so many startled, silt-colored birds.

COMMONALGIA

Alison Granucci

When I was ten, I started a nature club. I had barely made it
through fifth grade as the shy new kid trying to make friends
at a new school—but somehow I got six girls to come and I
led them on a wildflower walk pointing out all the common
weeds growing along the roadside. It was a success! So, with
an unfamiliar confidence, I assigned everyone to write a report
about a favorite flower or bird. At our next meeting, I read mine
about the red-winged blackbird I was in love with. Unbelieving
that I'd been serious about homework, all the girls quit. I was
instantly a club of one.

there's an erosion
as it's common to overlook, ignore
the numbers of common birds
and not common practice to count
19 common species
our taken-for-granted favorite birds
have each lost
their once-common communal flight
more than 50 million birds since 1970
can now hardly be found —
sparrows, warblers, finches, and
our common ground is losing ground
blackbirds were particularly hard hit
look at the unraveling
when you lose a common species
in our common skies

the impact
just look up and what you can't see
will be much more massive
will be nothing so common as a bird

In my 40s, I moved to the Hudson Valley from Vermont where
I had lived for eighteen years near a cattail-ringed pond, a
common nesting site for red-wings. Every spring I would
observe them from eggs to fledglings. In my new town, I didn't
see a blackbird for years but didn't give it a thought, as I was no
longer living near a wetland. More recently, as I started writing
about birds, rekindling my younger passion, I learned about the
decline of songbirds: how, in a single lifetime, my beloved spark-
bird had diminished by 92 million. I had to put down my pen.

a personal feeling of abandonment
an all too common grief, caused by the degradation
among our most common species
of their once abundant habitats
the sense of desolation connected to
Nature's shift from commonplace to collapse —
it's staggering
its distress is disaster:
the present state of one's home and territory
when protecting Nature is not common nature
when your sense of place is under attack
and even birdsong is on the decline —
(this continent has lost 3 billion birds)
what is the common cry of dying passerines
these are the birds we know and love
we need a New Book of Uncommon Prayer,

colorful and filled with song
litanies to restore our loss of common sense
in a much-loved place being desolated
sing: Our common earth is our common wealth!

Unbelievably, as I wrote this piece, a punk flock of sixty red-winged blackbirds with starlings and grackles swirled in with the late winter snow and landed on my deck, all squawk and bluster. My first sighting in twenty years. Joy! Each *conk-a-ree* said *long time, no see!*, every voice united and rising in a clarion call.

Then they took to the sky.

LIFE AS A GROUSE

Brandon Meland

You'll find them dumbfounded,
perhaps that they've made it this far,

or maybe perpetually in awe
of their changing environment.

You'll find them in the wilderness—
under brush or in a tree,

depending on their mood.
Always hiding.

Then sometimes,
when the conditions are right,

they expose themselves.
You'll see them on the edges of roads,

opening up, being vulnerable, being
momentarily free.

And before they have time to wonder: why
did the grouse cross the road?

BLAM!
The death flutter.

There's an easy way
to clean a grouse.

A way that makes the whole bird
come apart in one tugging motion.

Their wings pinned under boots,
their legs pulled by raw hands.

Their whole soft bodies torn from them,
leaving only what can be consumed.

Except the wings,
which are clipped later.

Isn't that just like a creature?
To discover, only when it's too late,

its fragility, its too-simple way of being
undone.

SIGNPOST

Jessica Simmons

Today I parked at a four-way
stop when a crow stepped out
in the lane next to me. He ventured
without looking to retrieve
a stringy worm, eyeing me as if to speak,
daring me to risk my life whatever
it may be.

THE SWALLOWS RETURN TO EAST 28TH STREET

Patrick Hansel

Not with trumpets, or portents or exactitude,
as at San Juan Capistrano, where the winged
heralds arrive right on time for St. Joseph's
Day, two days before spring. Nor in a whirl
of wings at dusk on the soccer pitch, phantoms
skimming inches above the grass, as my long-
legged daughter sprints goalward. The swallows
do not *arrive* at the old church tower on East
28th Street. They *appear*. One morning, they
are there, as I walk bottles and cans to the
recycling bin; one night, as spring stretches
its tongue over the long, dying winter, and
awakes joy, they are simply there. They are
there, skirting in and out of the cornices,
the nooks where their sisters, the sparrows,
have founded a nest to lay their young. They are
there, dwelling high enough above the thawing
earth to shield their eggs and hatchlings from
raccoon and rat, yet tucked into corners where
the tower meets the arched roof, tidy avian
hermitages too small for the red-tailed hawk—
that fierce remainder of souls—to enter and
plunder. The swallows return to East 28th Street,
not by clockwork nor command. They appear,
they tarry, they praise. Their wings whisper
each summer twilight. And then, of a season,

they are gone. Not having flown away; or departed;
but simply—and unnoticed for a time—they are
absent, as fall falls slowly towards another winter
and leaves us with just a slight rift in the sky,
where all our longings for birth, for rest seek shelter.

SOME CHICKEN

Kaylee Basel

Stuck in those barnyard blues again,
me and my chicken-kin. Cooped
and souped up with hay fresh-laid
and all that scattered food in the dirt,
one might even claim
we are sick, selfish chickens
just for feeling this way.

Still, we stay. Stuck
as if our claws and hooves
have been planted, permanent. Stuck
in those red, white and
blues. The horses too. But food
never runs out for us and the old, aching
fellow fills our buckets each day to the brim.

Never going thirsty—
never going anywhere, really.

Still anyway, we pass the time
and our bodies stay warm while we do.
And sometimes at dusk, when a storm
settles into a drizzle,
then into nothing but a misting dew,
its droplets land on the spider's web.
As if her prey, dancing and dousing, as if
her web is swallowed by diamonds

turned yellow from the fellow's
front porch light.

How can such a gentle mist
weigh so heavy on her glassy thread?

I know she will always start over
and spin another for my gaze.
And I know, again, the clouds will rain.
And with hay piled this high I question

if the layers burying me are made
of shredded bedding
or my own body. Does it matter?
Looking down from this coop that is mine,
with my belly full of feed and my blood
warm, everyone sleeps— but the spider.

The silent haze makes it seem
that it's just the two of us now.
The spider, never growing tired.
Me, never going anywhere. The barnyard
blues could never turn me blue
enough to part ways
with those gleaming, gold drops
in the unspoken show she labors over-
on nights like these-

just for me.

SONG

UNTITLED

Barry MacDonald

This moment can be a seed of joy if
I follow what a crow is doing on
a branch and I notice it's bobbing on
one of the upper branches just as if
it's claiming a prominent perch as if
it's exerting a dominance upon
this little territory whereupon
it's bobbing and it's cawing in a riff
of abrasive assaultive utterance
while I don't see any other bird or
squirrels in the surrounding trees or on
the ground as it's casting a wary glance
around — I don't know what it is cawing for
and can't imagine what it's set upon.

Whatever the crow
was doing is beyond my
knowing as the world
is mysterious and now

the crow has moved somewhere else.

HOW TO BE A BIRD

Julia Klatt Singer

Let yourself be
drawn to the shape of wings; how they hold
the light, become the patterns
You dream.

Know the world
through your eyes and your ears. Give in
to the pull of the earth, and what moves
beneath you.

Find you balance
with your hips
Hunt by feel.
Let the sun
lead you.

You will lighten
and streamline your body.
Map the air's heat and scents.
To travel means flight.

Sing for the love of it.
Feed your lover.
Feast and forage.

CALL AND RESPONSE HAIKU

Rebecca Paradis

Thunder! Turkeys gobble-

Rooster reports he also

Is loud -repeat-

A GANNET NAMED NIGEL

Morus serrator
Nigel—The Washington Post by Karin Brulliard, February 6, 2018
Amelia Díaz Ettinger

should i be sad for Nigel
maybe bellow his loss?

he loved a cement
gannet for all of his life

she was a decoy
a lure to bring more of his kind

and yet, for years he was faithful
he gave her fish and renovated their nest

she was everything for him season after season
his silent companion on an empty rocky shore

while her paint faded and no other gannets met
he waited by her side

for the sound of her and others
was his song different then in this void?

did he sing his throaty vibrato?
or did he wait to be far at sea to screech?

i don't know these things
but I know something about his seclusion

too afraid to venture far
now i live with decoys—images that talk inside of boxes

where i share a few fragments
in the safety of these flat screens

like Nigel—

i feed my solitude the best I can
try to find faith in a setting sun

while i cling to this hope—
a world full of gannets and their full song

THIS YOUNG CROW CALLS TO LIVE

Timothy Young

It's midnight. A fledgling crow
caws from the cornfield. It's a strong call.
Last week it cried hoarsely,
and inadequately
from deep inside the tree grove.

By Friday it reached the grove's edge
and raucous, older crows
spent the day encouraging it on.
Now, the young one calls to live,
all day and half the night.

Earlier today it's great demand
rose from the corn rows
the way vapor would
to become a cloud for serious
thunder and lightning.

In the dark the crow
has to look up through
the tall maize and wonder,
when and how he'll reach the stars
that glow beyond the silk tassels.

WOODPECKERS

Alamgir Hashmi

Their flight paths are hardly known
but they first alight on the house wall,
then the wooden railing, and one by one
step up to the outer door of my father's
room; knock, knock, knock.
One of them turns around, flies back
up the wall. The other one,
just the same restless stripe—
a warm brown, gray, black-white;
gets back the same tapping sound
from the shut door—ticktock peck,
skilling patience to flying
an angle of possible sight.
The third watches
through the rush of this moment
set deep in the wall,
his eye amused, his feathers aflutter.
Meanwhile, these two look at each other
and the door with no one in view,
fly into the next guava tree
by the look-alike house door,
its answering silence, or perhaps more.

AGAIN THE DOVES IN THE TIME OF THE PANDEMIC

Diane Jarvenpa

I have been hearing mourning doves,
what is it about their calls
that rescue a frenetic mind?

The song's slow beat insists a mellow-out
as if Donovan was singing from some rooftop
or the same way when Ray Charles offers, as only he can,

Oh What A Beautiful Morning with the Count Basie Orchestra,
there is no way you can refute that slow melodic truth.
If any directive can be found from doves

it is—make do, keep going. I do find endearing
their *Whatever man,* approach to life.
Nests made up anywhere, telephone poles will do.

But their flight, all purpose in sudden ascent or dodge,
most needed now. They survive in desert, drink brackish water,
live almost as long as Jesus, though this is unlikely.

Twenty million are hunted every year.
I find a weird hope in their returning here, a comfort in their deep
allowance for approximation. Their song sounds a lament,

maybe hunger or emergence of egg
or maybe not alarm or complaint.
I admit as I field their susurration

into my very tired brain, I nod to their sigh
of plausibility for something more than a slim wedge of hope,
for how indeed, *the sounds of the earth are like music.*

MOCKINGBIRD

Michael Kiesow Moore

Would you like being born without your own song?
What would you do if you had mostly gray feathers,
not any of the braggart orange of the Baltimore oriole,
nor even the accenting red dot of a cedar waxwing?
So much of our own we lay on certain ones.
"If you don't like my wren, let me show you my
German shepherd, my Persian cat. Or how about
wind chimes, or a car alarm?"
Everyone wants attention.
Isn't that what love is?

BLACKBIRD IN BELOIT

Jim Rogers

The guide book gets some of it right,
though omits how the bird shrugs its wings,
enlarging to flash his gold-edged, scarlet epaulets.
The book neglects the reddening willow switches
or the residuum of last year's swamp, reeds
bending over and fat cattail heads
now crumbling into grains, like pollen.

But the book comes close on the call:
"A gurgling *oak-a-lee*, followed by *chek*."

All the same, paper only takes you so far.
So much more is being said when,
on a concrete path beside the Rock River
a Redwing ejaculates its spring-loaded song:
that the earth is always a woman,
and that somehow, somewhere,
and in important ways, we get this wrong.

DAWN CHORUS

Sabrina Kirby

What I took for the chickadee's
hey, sweetie in the dark hemlock
unfurls in Palmer cursive
into hermit thrush morning song.

Brown headed cowbird's
shrill liquid bell rasp
like stolen drops of blue jay chatter.

I struggle to love the cowbird
who lays her eggs in others' nests
and returns on the sly to feed
her precocious murderous hatchlings
so once grown, they may recognize
their future mates.
All beings want to live.

Now the cardinal appears
black against brightening sky
right here right here right here
and layers its clear voice
under others I thought I knew.

It was the hermit thrush I longed for,
my ear that embellished the chickadee's song.
See how I grasp.
I grasp and grasp.
Have I learned nothing?

First light of morning,
be my breath.
Make of this wanting
a waiting.
Make of this waiting
a green darkness.
Make of this darkness
a cool space, a palm extended
Make of this palm
an empty perch—

CATBIRD

Thomas R. Smith

Often you'll find him
hiding near the heart of a tree.
He likes to be heard, but isn't
keen on being seen.
His song says it's
sweet to be a shadow.

All poets who love variety
should hold him dear.
A little Neruda, a little
Yeats, a lot of
Mary Oliver — it's all
there in his melody.

Poets, take a lesson
from the catbird:
Step back on the branch a bit
closer to the trunk—
there you'll be steady—
and sing.

LAST VESTIGES

Kathryn Reilly

wanting,
she descends gnarled branches
stretching wings in starlight
greeting dawn's first rays
still waters ripple and
her song haunts
the newborn morning
seeking her own kind
living in ephemeral hope

the world stills
lamenting her sadness

she persists
morning mists wrapping her harmonies
in memory
settling her song down
down to dew-kissed grasses

her sadness cascades and stutters the song
feathered and scaled and furred and amphibious
neighbors caress her voice with their own
creating a chorus reminding
lonely yet not alone

in inflicted solitude
she waits
for the fading of her light

LOONS

D.E. Green

The loons are at it again
in the middle of the night:
hooting and quarreling,

moaning their joy and pain,
cawing commands,
shrieking like Shakespearean shrews.

I wake, worry the sheets,
toss off the twisted covers,
turn, slip under again—

sleep on edge, anticipate
the night's shrill keening.

HAIKU FOR THE BIRDS

Fiona McNabb

Crows, all in a murder,
dance over rooftops, calling —
almonds for the fowl!

THE SONG OF THE COMMON SPARROW

Carol Rucks

Inside the stiff branches
of an arborvitae
gray sparrows huddle and sing.
The snow falls steadily down,
bringing more cold and cruelty.
I stop to listen
as they rush through
the Hallelujah Chorus, the most
cheerful thing hidden in plain sight.
If I loiter here too long
they'll stop, go shy,
and flutter away.

HOPE AND BIRDSONG

Dougie Padilla

yes, when i am gone from here,
i'll send word from the other side.

and it will sound like birdsong, my friend,
every note of these birds singing, singing...
an old soul just trying to ring us hello.

hello? hello? anyone there?

yes, when i am gone from here,
i'll send word from the other side.

and it will sound like birdsong

BIRD SPIRIT MAN GOD

Patrick Hansel

God fears us all
Theresa Svoboda

I woke early to beat the birds
to song. I lost. The sky shed
its darkness like skin. I sat.
Above the reach of the shagbark
maple, a royal butterfly floated,
its wings whispered wind. My voice

is bark, roughed to keep dreams
in, to keep bugs out, but today
I cannot see where I am growing.
Life, this bark of spirit we wear,
is true and not true in the same
breath—whether we sing paeans,
to the sun or dirges bent down low,

we are all held in our voices.

I will sing. I will trumpet
the name of heaven before
I surrender, I will go down
singing. There is no fear
but the one we lack a name for,
the face that stares and will not speak,
the one that walks in me each day,

and yet,

like greening leaves, like
wings, I turn to beg the sun to sing
to this earth. I am the spade,
the rake, the borrowed
glory of ancient vowels.
I have a remnant word to lift up.
Sing with me, doves and robins.
Dive into my voice
and find a worm, a seed
just right for plucking,
for flying home to bestow
upon your chirping offspring.

SO BE IT

Mike Hazard

Cheered by, I cheered
a cheery robin, cheering
at the top of his voice,
atop an antenna
atop our neighbor's home.
The bird was singing
to the moon, rising.
I joined in, humming
along, a duet.
If this is the end of time
so be it.

SPRING GARDEN

Alison Granucci

Before any green's revealed, a rush
of birds open and close the day with song

while in between   the world lives
and dies   and grows   as Spring comes

winging in on the warbling   *wheee-IT*
whistling   *wheee-IT*   syrinxes of sound.

Softly mourning, the dove's *cooAH-coo* coaxes
newly stirring roots   while Crow's raw *CAW-*

CAW   calls to all quiescent shoots   to cleave
the cusp of earth, revive its sylvan skin.

We're here! declares the chick-*a-dee-dee*,
the chattering of the jay, and the drumming

on a trunk — each beat   each note
a cadence   exhorting the eager dirt —

for what stretch   what push   what yield
WHA-cheer   WHA-cheer -cheer

must occur to *teew-teew-teew* loosen
the enduring dark of winter's incubation?

O the things the ground must know
that all the gods do not! *Hip-churr-eeh*

sings a song sparrow to the snowdrop —
milky blossomed herald of March —

you show us   again   the soil
always surrenders to the shoot.

A flock of titmice fluster in to *tsay tsay*:
Look *he-ere* at this red trillium

trilling red, this wood poppy   popping yellow!
Look down, down at this daffadowndilly —

Spring cannot *kee-ep-her* long in the ephemeral
garden — each second   *he-ere* fades

with a bloom, each bloom   *he-ere*   dies
into day, each day   *he-ere*   is counted down

by the constant bob   of the phoebe tail . . .

WHAT THE BIRDS SAID TODAY

Greg Watson

Just start singing,
they seemed to say.
The words will
come in time,
and with the words
their meaning.

NEST

ROBIN

Carol Rucks

Half way up
to the squirrels' nest
she sits in a clutch
of dreams.
A heated stillness
slows the wind.
Her circle of gathered
sticks and seeds
pockets the darkness.

THE FEEDER

Fiona McNabb

I watch and wait for her to go
the crow who tore my feathered tail
she stuffs the nuts into her throat
I watch and wait for her to go
the wind is fast the rain is slow
the swaying branches softly wail
I watch and wait for her to go
the crow who tore my feathered tail

PELICAN

Dougie Padilla

pelican on the water
out beyond the spring ice
right there exactly
where the sun dissolves
into a stretch of silver light.

such a long, skinny neck!

PILIATED WOODPECKER

Dryocopus pileatus
Amelia Díaz Ettinger

most likely a mating dance
or just 'stay with me for this season'

to witness is a gift,
a dance up and down a grand fir

turned Maypole for this dramatic duo
red crest aflame and uncommonly quiet

nothing of their raucous *kik — kikkik*
no drumming on bark to wake this forest

no—a silent dance of black and red feathers up
and down　　　　　prehensile tails make it possible

to stand with frozen wingbeats
longing stares　　　　　white underwings

adverted from everyone else's vision
just each other exist in this private ritual

what is it like to move so freely in the open,
pirouetting in fevered sunshine?

what is it like to keep view of your lover,
even if it's only for one more summer?

WHITE PELICANS

Jim Lenfestey

The word went out among the white
pelican community of the Dakotas:
The Holocaust of DDT has ended!

And so...
back to the tumble of Pelican Rapids,
the sand of St. Croix beaches,
the solace of Cedar Lake,
the roosts on rocky islets in Green Bay.

Bigger than browns, jet black melanin-
stiffened tips of white flight feathers
soared home with a graceful softness
we had not the wisdom to remember
we had missed.

TREE ON A HILL:
MARINE-ON-ST.-CROIX, MINNESOTA

D.E. Green

You're both mass and grace
your boll turned slightly at the base

like a dancer in mid-pivot.
Your limbs, three large stems at

chin-level, arch over the hill, rise up
and overlook the slope.

One seems as if it's glancing
back, casting behind a longing

lingering look. There's a silent strength to you,
your leaves barely stirring in the cool

of the mid-spring breeze after a cold
rain. A robin is flitting, bold,

out in the sunlight on the lawn
that extends to the pond, fringed

with dried cattails along the water's edge.
The red breast is roused, then gone

up the hill through your limbs.
I am sitting a few feet from him

as he flies by. I would welcome
your solidity, your calm—

to be open to a robin
flashing through outstretched
arms to the sun beyond.

UNDESIRABLE

MaryAnn Franta Moenck

His loud crowing, his sharp spurs,
his girth crowding the perch.
Legs thick, feathers black.
Iridescent—
The man who said he'd take him
before winter has not called.

Cockiness can lead to
Coq au Vin. His tall comb
subject to frostbite.
His flap and strut and bluster.
The kick and dance just before
he ravishes a hen half his size.

Murmuring swagger
as he rounds up the flock,
his hackles flare at some unseen
predator. He blinks, suspicious
at my approach, knows
I won't take his guff.

The man hasn't called—
I offer a bit of cheddar
from my palm. He tilts an eye,
lifts the morsel, softly
drops it before the smallest hen.
His toenails ivory, soles bright gold.

COASTAL DRIVE

Donna Isaac

after "Postscript" by Seamus Heaney

And very soon travel three miles out

From Mobile Bay across a long bridge

Out to Dauphin Island in the Gulf

Low tide when the grey water pulls

Away from this barrier, the dune

Wind frilling sea oats, bitter beachgrass

Where pied oysterbirds ply long

Orange beaks diving deep into the hearts

Of bivalves slightly open to the air.

These long-legged, knobby-kneed birds dart bright eyes

Keen to the bounty revealed by receding wave

Piping in tandem their high shrill sound

Joining a chorus of plovers, pipers, sanderlings,

Great blue herons, white egrets, spring migrators

In sanctuary. To be a witness of such winged beauty

On this isle still surviving saltwater rise!

MY GRANDMOTHER'S CHILDHOOD

Jim Rogers

In each paintless Kentucky
village of her youth,

she cried when wanton
boys turned birds' nests

into litter. Bluebird chicks
spilled as from a kicked bucket

and were left to squall, their helpless
chirps lasting the afternoon.

Eggs splattered
like tobacco-spit on a rock.

She wept and was told
there was nothing to weep for.

The boys were only birding.

THE ROBIN BUILDS HER CORONA NEST

Patrick Hansel

It rained last night—peals
of thunder before dawn—
so fat worms should be ripe
for picking. But this mother-to-be
only looks for the best tufts of
brown grass. She plucks a
beakful, flies to the elbow joint
of the downspout where she
is building a crown for her brood.
She places the fibers in the bowl,
then butts it all down, her soft
rear welcoming each strand.
Six feet is the proscribed distance
for creatures under threat,
but there is good bedding near
my feet and so she dives to gather
what the earth is sloughing off,
then rises to add this treasure
to the new house. Soon, it will be
a cup for the sky blue eggs she
now wombs, a crown for her to wear
upside down, her soft bum a gentle
warmth to her offspring, a welcome
of new life to this quaking land.

BLACKBIRD AND THE MEADOW

Michael S. Moos

The blackbird glides in low, disappears into the glistening
early slough grass, starting back to life.
For a little while, not happy. Just content. Peaceful breaths.
No fear of anything.
Even the grass rises, falls in a kind of breathing.
Forget all the rhetorics, the mechanics of the day waiting
in the brittle stalks of dried cattails.
There will be enough other days to pay back futility,
that approximation of change. To recall waking in the night,
in love with the waning moon off in its endless dark.
You have this small room of time to listen to the world, to resist
fear and failing, something coming down like dark wings.
Listen, says the heart. Wade across the river, says the mind.
Carry the patient body into the sunlight, taste the salt
disappearing from pain. It is that simple, says the body.
As if death praises the simple acts.
The recollection of breaking out of one small world into another.
Lungs rising, as if they hold the memory of the sea.

UNTITLED

Barry MacDonald

He is clever to shake his tail feathers
the air is filled with potent vibrations
the peacock is a tricky romancer

the feathers express the male's intentions
his frequency tickles the peahen's crest
the hen and cock vibrate in unison

flamboyance enhances the peacock's quest
he displays his fan of dozens of eyes
it's no wonder the hen becomes possessed

the peacock is lusty and wins his prize
the pageantry of earth is astounding
a panoply of eyes will mesmerize

the scope of design is hypnotizing
the patterns of life are captivating.

A BLUEBIRD OF HAPPINESS

Mike Hazard

A bluebird of happiness flies
in Geraldine's aquamarine eyes.
I feared she'd died and flown
to heaven when I found her,
here in this rest home since
she can't remember when.
She's good on the old days,
not so on the current questions
she repeats like bird calls.
Are you a good husband?
Are you a good husband?
I answer you're my teacher
in the school of hard knocks.
She says her daughter once
spelled that knocks "k.n.o.x.".
Giving her a little peck goodbye,
I flutter away, stopping to study
the bluebird picture by her door.
In Geraldine's aquamarine eyes
a bluebird of happiness flies.

IN PRAISE OF CROWS

Rev. Ted Tollefson

Crows are holding a conference call
from the tree-tops this morning
and there's a dispute going on
about who didn't share yesterday's road-kill
or who took more than their fair-share.

Crows, it's worth noting
like early Christians
share "all things in common" as St. Paul says
including opinions
which they share freely and at length.

Everybody knows they're our recycling crew
who offer loud prayers over
whatever they find
like priests doing their rounds
at nursing homes.

But have you noticed
they also give advance warning
of anything unexpected in the 'hood—
a strange car on the road,
a door left open too late
or someone who does not belong
nosing around an empty house.

Though crows will never gain respect
like their upper class Eagle cousins

we depend upon them utterly
and could offer some words
of long overdue praise
for those who clean up our messes
and embody such crafty generosity.

THE CANADA GEESE SHOW

Michael Kiesow Moore

I watched a flock of Canada geese swim just off the shoreline.
When I first looked out I saw a perfect V, as if they were in flight,
a leader at the apex and the rest floating by in their two lines.
The group slowly meandered north. Next time I looked,
they were back, now ambling southward.
The last time I remembered to look their way
I saw them all swimming single file—heading north again—
a conga line of Canada geese, as if they said,
"Now watch this!" If we could see the feet,
it might look like a Can Can, all the webbed
feet circling in unison below the surface.

SNAG TREE

Kathryn Reilly

the argument warbles over morning coffee:
she wants the tree to stay
he wants the tree down, roots ground to mulch;
ultimately, she wins and ten feet remain
in their suburban backyard

the trunk weathers four seasons,
bark loosening
polypores rooting
and crawling tenants arrive
finding refuge in wooden death;
decay sustains many tiny lives:
termites and ant armies and
wood boring beetles
and carpenter bees and

patiently, she waits
soon afterward
her reward arrives
sounding staccato rhythms
to celebrate the morning

pilated woodpecker pairs
tails balancing, talons anchoring
prepare for sharp beak's breach
tap, tap, tap into the trunk
pausing to trill their delight
crimson crests catch sunlight

feasting, round and round they go
in tandem hunting, extracting, relishing
repeat. repeat. repeat. repeat.
working together they tunnel in,
creating crevices for smaller creatures
(eventually, a downy woodpecker nests here)

sated, the pairs retreat
bold black and white feathers
disappearing through the trees
dozens of tiny holes and several larger ones
beckon to new chitinous homesteaders

the snag tree stands
life-giving for many years to come

HUMMINGBIRD PRISM

Becky Boling
A duplex after Jericho Brown

The hummingbird doesn't hover but hangs, an ornament.
Stained-glass wings framed in metal are frozen in place.

Outlined in metal the hummingbird wings are frozen
as if about to sip at blooms on the other side of the window.

Outside the window, bursting blooms guard their nectar
from the caged hummingbird's thirsty glass beak.

The hummingbird thirsts for sweetness in his glass cage
within the curved metal frame, thinks of dancing branches

dreams tree limbs dancing in wind. The bird perches.
Sunlight flits through blue-green, red panes of glass.

Flitting blue-green, red sunlight through glass panes
throws prismatic glances on bare white walls.

Prismatic shards of light pitched on bare white walls
the hummingbird doesn't hover but hangs, an ornament.

LORD TOM

Rebecca Paradis

The biggest tom turkey unfurls
On the runway of Shady Lane,
A step –a slow spin- finding
The best light, he shimmers,
Rattling his feathery jewels,
Thrusting his blue and red head
At hens and bully toms
That dash past, he is
Lord Of The Road
And The Sun Shining On It.

A neighbor returns home,
Bigger, shinier, louder,
Not slowing down,
Tom folds up shop and
Relinquishes the runway.
With a smooth exit to the wings,
He blends in with the foraging flock.

WHILE THE WREN BUILDS HIS NEST

MaryAnn Franta Moenck

Small brown bird, have me for your song.
Perched on your tiny house,
while I for an hour pretend attention

to other things, you call out
all for love. *Come see what I've made,*
what I am making just for you.

Each stick you bring to furnish the space,
then hop to the roof, announce success,
another twig placed just so.

Your throat swells with love-song,
a fluttering lodged in my heart. Green
all around us blooms into blush

and I feign to not care. Then there's a hush
and I prize the silence, anticipate—
all yours as I wait

to hear you (no matter it's not for me) —
sing again.

THE OWL GODS

Dougie Padilla

i had an art world zoom meeting last night
to discuss career opportunities for artists.
for a while i thought there were birds,
probably grackles, scratching at my ears,
pecking at them, pecking hard.

don't worry, they didn't get to my ear drums,
tho i had to fight them off for a good while.
i'm gonna head out of town now before
reinforcements show and the battle
goes downhill and there's blood and bleeding
and all things mercenary.

maybe instead i'll head out to the far reaches
on my new as yet unused snowshoes,
great metal bird feet for the long marches i crave,
the day long rambles thru deep white woods
in search of great horned owls, great gray owls, screech
owls (both red and gray), barred owls, snowy owls, northern
saw-whet owls, short-eared owls, long-eared owls or
maybe even a barn owl tho i'm hearing they're getting
scarce and are mostly found much further south of here.

i figure, best to head up into the bluffs for a week or two,
never moving, soft and fluid of mind and body,
way beyond alert, open to the gods,
open to the owls and the owl gods
and then they will show. maybe.

DOWN TO EARTH

Diane Jarvenpa

Robins are everywhere now, in the streets, in the elms,
dead in my hands.

The sky split and sent a male robin into the side of the house,
there in the grass, pristine,

just the way you'd find one in a natural history museum,
well-groomed, not stuffed,

but newly empty. And an instinct to will it
back to life takes over,

which chants to offer which deity, what wound
can be healed with doubt?

If I believed in reincarnation, maybe I was holding
a beautiful Bolivian farmer, Athabascan weaver,

innkeeper at the edge of Lake Baikal, or once an ant, a worm
    best eaten.
Who is to say connectors of worlds don't have brown wings

that settle onto a spirit tree like papery blooms?
We never know the many ghosts that hover,

how grief spurs a different calculation as we try to hold onto
a story even when it has cast off its own ending.

Hollow bones are swept back to earth
each time I bury a bird,

offered to yet one more holy landscape
of loss and red clover.

TO THE TREEPIES OF NORTHERN INDIA

Greg Watson

This, then, must be the true nature of
prayer: a pure, clawing hunger

that brings you swooping down
to steal from the stone temple walls

those small votive candles
burning brightly with butter fat.

With a knowing tilt of your head,
the flame gives itself up to the wind,

a motion hardly noticed by
the devout or those simply passing.

Who could question such unwavering
devotion, bowing and returning

throughout the bright dust of daylight?
Who could dismiss the need for sustenance

as mere thievery, the insistence of the
body as anything but sacred?

We fold our hands merely to mimic
the oneness of your form,

chant for hours merely to emulate
the purity of your song;

longing all the while to be wrapped
in a single shroud of sky.

We are humble guests, forever so,
in this home you have created.

Brilliant scavenger, fire eater,
unrepentant survivor, take what you need.

The gods will not mind.
They have all the light in the world.

NEST

Rob Hardy

I keep thinking today
will be different:
the poem I write
will have long lines
and won't refer to itself.
It will reach out its long arms
to embrace the world.
My poem won't be about birds,
but the birds themselves
will carry my poem,
line by line,
to build their nests.
The oriole will lay her eggs
in my poem—
ink-scribbled,
parchment-colored eggs,
like the fragments
of some medieval manuscript.
But there will be no similes
in my poem—
only the oriole herself
and her fragile eggs.

ABOUT THE CONTRIBUTORS

Kaylee Basel

Kaylee Basel is a poet and professional in higher education from Boston, Massachusetts. She earned her Bachelor of Fine Arts with a focus in Poetry in 2019. She recently graduated in May of 2022 as a Master of Fine Arts in Poetry from Emerson College, where she taught writing throughout her graduate career.
She now works as a Program Coordinator in the Writing and Academic Resource Center at Emerson College. "Some Chicken" is a featured piece from her MFA manuscript titled "The Tour". Much of her work deals with themes of social and familial responsibility, favors the art of description and honors the urban landscapes in and around Boston.

Becky Boling

Becky Boling has published creative nonfiction, dramatic monologues, short stories and poetry (*The Ekphrastic Review, Lost Lake Folk Opera, Willows Wept Review, Persimmon Tree, 3rdWednesday Magazine*). Her poems have won competitions— Northfield Sidewalk Poetry & Red Wing Arts' Poet-Artist Collaboration (2020, 2022) and she has twice been nominated for a Pushcart Prize. A retired professor (Carleton College), she concentrates on creative writing these days. Firmly rooted, like dandelions, in Minnesota soil, she attributes her small successes to her live-in editor, D. E. Green, as well as fellow writers in her writing groups.

"Owls" has been published previously in Willows Wept Review

Amelia Diaz Ettinger

Amelia Díaz Ettinger is a Latinx BIPOC poet and writer. Her published books include *Learning to Love a Western Sky* by Airlie Press, a bilingual book of poetry, *Speaking at a Time /Hablando a la Vez* by Redbat Press, and a chapbook, *Fossils in a Red Flag* by Finishing Line Press. A forthcoming poetry collection, *Between the Eyes of the Lizard and the Moon*, will be published by Redbat Press. Amelia's poetry and short stories have been published in anthologies, literary magazines, and periodicals.

She has an MS in Biology and MFA in creative writing. Her literary work is a marriage of science and her experience as an immigrant. Presently, she resides in Eastern Oregon.

MaryAnn Franta Moenck

MaryAnn Franta Moenck is the author of Bees in the Attic, Finishing Line Press, 2014. Her poems have appeared in Dogwood, Snowy Egret, Cimarron Review, Nimrod, and Water~Stone Review. She participated in the 2012-2013 Loft Mentor Series. MaryAnn lives with her husband on a small acreage above the beautiful Saint Croix River valley in western Wisconsin, where she enjoys gardening, foraging, and fiber arts.

"Undesirable" first appeared online in Half Way Down the Stairs, December 2022, ed. Jeannie E. Roberts and Phillip Watts Brown, https://halfwaydownthestairs.net/ and is published here with permission.

Alison Granucci

Granucci has been a bird lover since she can remember and in college, she trained as a naturalist. In 2005, she founded the literary speaker's agency, Blue Flower Arts, and ran it for 15 years before retiring. For the past two years she has been immersed in writing about birds, poetry and prose, under the guidance of Chip Blake, former editor of Orion magazine and Milkweed Press. Her work has been published, or is forthcoming, in EcoTheo Review and Great River Review.

D.E. Green

D.E. (Doug) Green taught English at Augsburg University for 33 years. He has published articles on Shakespeare, general-interest essays, and poetry. His poem "Gratitude" won the 2018 *Martin Lake Journal* Bookend Prize; other work has appeared in *Bright Light: Stories in the Night* (Southeastern Minnesota Poets, 2021 and 2022); in the 2021 and 2022 Red Wing Arts Poet Artist Collaboration; in *Third Wednesday*; in *Lost Lake Folk Opera*; in *Willows Wept Review*; and on the sidewalks of his hometown, Northfield, Minnesota. Three of his poems were recognized in the 2022 League of Minnesota Poets Contest. His first collection, *Jumping the Median*, was published in 2019 by Encircle Publications. Doug likes to say that he has been an occasional poet for 40 years.

"Loons" and "The Would-be Naturalist Goes Birding" appear in the 2019 collection, *Jumping the Median*. "Tree on a Hill" appeared in *Bright Light: Stories in the Night* in 2021

Patrick Hansel

Patrick Cabello Hansel is the author of the poetry collections *The Devouring Land* (Main Street Rag Publishing) and *Quitting Time* (Atmosphere Press) and *Breathing in Minneapolis* (Finishing Line Press, November 2023). He has published poems and prose in over 85 journals, including *Crannog, Ilanot Review, North Dakota Quarterly, Water-Stone Review* and *Lunch Ticket*. Nominated three times for a Pushcart Prize, he has won awards from the Loft Literary Center and MN State Arts Board. He is the editor of *The Phoenix of Phillips*, a literary journal by and for the most diverse community in Minneapolis. His website is: www. artecabellohansel.com

"Bird Spirit Man God" was published in *The Closed Eye Open*

"Bath Time for the Robins, St. Luke's Day, October 18" was published in the *Crossings Art Center Poet-Artist Collaboration Series*

"The Swallows Return to East 28th Street" was published in the Anthology *Goodness*

"The Robin Builds Her Corona Nest" was published in *Thema*

Rob Hardy

Rob Hardy lives in Northfield, Minnesota, where since 2016 he has served as the city's first Poet Laureate. He's the author of a full-length poetry collection, *Domestication* (2017), and two poetry chapbooks, *The Collecting Jar* (2005) and *Shelter in Place* (2022). His writing, both poetry and prose, has appeared in numerous literary magazines and anthologies, including the

2008 *Best of the Net*. He has collaborated with composer Alex Freeman on several choral works, including a choral symphony, that received their premiere in 2022 in Helsinki, Finland.

"Sparrows" originally appeared in *Willows Wept Review*

"Good Friday Walk" originally appeared in *Poetic Strokes*

"Nest" originally appeared in *West Branch*

Alamgir Hashmi

Alamgir Hashmi is the author of numerous books of poetry and literary criticism. His poetry and prose have also appeared widely in journals and anthologies (the latest being *Wild Gods* from New Rivers Press, 2021) and won him high honors. He has taught as a university professor and is Founding President of The Literature Podium: An Independent Society for Literature and the Arts.

Mike Hazard

Mike Hazard is a filmmaker, photographer, and poet. Nine of his films have been broadcast nationally on public media; 228 play on social media. His pictures are in many museums, including MOMA (NY). A collection of Hazard's poems about people, "This World Is Not Altogether Bad," is published by Red Dragonfly Press. The poet likes to say, "Everything I make is a love story." To learn more, visit: https://www.mikehazard.org/

Jaqi Holland

Jaqi Holland is a poet and essayist living in Salem, MA. She holds an M.A. in Writing & Publishing from Emerson College. Her work has appeared in *The Christian Science Monitor*, *The Ekphrastic Review*, *Brevity & Echo*, *Plenty Magazine*, *Humana Obscura*, and *Plant People: an Anthology of Environmental Artists*.

Donna Isaac

Poet Donna Isaac is a teaching artist and organizer of community readings/workshops through the League of MN Poets, the Cracked Walnut chapter, and co-hosts Literary Bridges, a reading series in St. Paul, MN. She has a B.A. from James Madison University; an M.A. from the University of Minnesota; and an M.F.A. from Hamline University. Published poetry work includes *Footfalls* (Pocahontas Press); *Tommy* (Red Dragonfly Press); *Holy Comforter* (Red Bird Chapbooks); and *Persistence of Vision* (Finishing Line Press), including many poems in literary journals. donnaisaacpoet.com

Diane Jarvenpa

Diane Jarvenpa is the author of *The Way She Told her Story*, *The Tender Wild Things* and *Divining the Landscape* - New Rivers Press and *swift, bright, drift* and *Ancient Wonders, The Modern World*- Red Dragonfly Press. She has received The Midwest Independent Publishers Association Award and an Artist Initiative grant from the Minnesota State Arts Board. She is a teaching artist with the Alzheimer's Poetry Project MN and was awarded one of the 50 over 50 Minnesotans for writing/music contributions in intergenerational communities by Pollen Midwest and AARPMN. She is a singer-songwriter performing under the name Diane Jarvi. www.dianejarvi.com

Sabrina Kirby

Kirby has recently re-committed to the practice of poetry after a twenty year pause, during which her creative energy went toward working with student and faculty writers in a university writing center. Before starting that full-time job, and after completing a post-grad semester at Vermont College, she was beginning to see her work published in small literary magazines such as *Acorn Whistle* and *Wind Magazine*.

Julia Klatt Singer

Julia Klatt Singer is a poet and painter from Minneapolis, Minnesota. She has four books of poetry, and her most recent work can be found at Autumn Sky Daily Poetry, The Saint Paul Almanac, and Silver Birch Press. She works at Grace Neighborhood Nursery School as their poet in residence. Audio poems from her most recent book, Elemental (Prolific Press) Poems written to the periodic table can be found at OpenKim. org, where she is the elemental, Sp, the element of surprise.

Jim Lenfestey

After a career in academia, marketing communications and journalism on the editorial board of the StarTribune, where he won several Page One awards for excellence, since 2000 Lenfestey has published two collections of personal essays, seven collections of poems, edited three poetry anthologies and co-edited *Robert Bly in This World*, University of Minnesota Press. His *haibun* memoir, *Seeking the Cave: A Pilgrimage to Cold Mountain* (Milkweed Editions) was a finalist for the 2014 Minnesota Book Award. His sixth poetry collection, *A Marriage*

Book: *50 Years of Poems from a Marriage* (Milkweed Editions), was a finalist for two 2017 Midwest Book Awards. In 2020 he received the Kay Sexton Award for significant contributions and leadership in the Minnesota Literary Community. For fifteen years he chaired the Literary Witnesses poetry program in Minneapolis and led a summer poetry class on Mackinac Island, Michigan. He lives in Minneapolis with his wife the political activist Susan Lenfestey. They have four children and eight grandchildren.

Barry MacDonald

Barry MacDonald goes by the *dharma* name "*Tekkan*," which means "Iron Man" in 12th century Japanese. *Tekkan* indicates a "settled practitioner of great determination." He was given the name when he took Buddhist vows. *Tekkan's* poetry is an exploration of everyday consciousness. He looks for inspiration in ordinary events. He lived in Japan for 9 years, teaching English at the Berlitz Corporation in Kyoto. He practiced at the Zen at *Hosshin-ji*, a Zen temple in Obama — a small town on the coast of the Sea of Japan.

Steven McCown

A Pushcart nominee, Steven McCown has published poems in *Lost Lake Folk Opera Magazine, Willows Wept Review, Colorado Crossing, Arizona Western Voice, Bright Lights Stories in the Night*, Minnesota Public Radio's End in Mind project, the 2023 *Red Wing Poet-Artist Collaboration*, as well as in *Legacies: Poetic Living Wills, Minnesota Writes, Minnesota Reads e-library*. His poem "The Bridge at Bridge Square" was included in *Northfield Poetry Tours: Poems about Northfield Places*. In 2020, his poetry collection

Ghosting was published by Shipwrect Publishing Company. After teaching high school and college English on the deserts of California and Arizona for over 30 years, McCown now lives in beautiful Northfield, Minnesota, where five of his poems are stamped in the sidewalks.

Dan McGleno

Dan McGleno is a St. Paul poet.

Fiona McNabb

Fiona McNabb studied English literature and writing at the University of Maryland, and is a graduate of the Jimenez-Porter Writers' House program.

Brandon Meland

Brandon lives in Minneapolis, MN. You can find some of his work in Band of Bards, The Bookends Review, and Rock, Paper Scissors. He holds an MFA in Creative Writing from Hamline University and is currently working on a novel about religious fundamentalism (but, like, the fun kind).

Michael Kiesow Moore

Michael Kiesow Moore lives in Saint Paul, Minnesota and is the author of the poetry collections *What to Pray For* and *The Song Castle* (Nodin Press). His work has appeared in many journals such as *International Times*, *Poetry City* and *Water~Stone Review*, anthologies like *Queer Voices, Among the Leaves: Queer Male Poets on the Midwestern Experience* and *A Loving Testimony: Losing Loved Ones Lost to AIDS*, and Garrison Keillor's "The Writer's

Almanac." Michael is the founder of the Birchbark Books Reading Series. www.michaelkiesowmoore.com

Michael Moos

Michael S. Moos has four poetry books, most recently *The Idea of the Garden* (winner of the Richard Snyder Poetry Prize from Ashland Poetry Press). He has received a number of national and regional poetry awards, has an MFA from Columbia University, and been a poet-in-residence for the Academy of American Poets. Recent poems have appeared in *Atlanta Review, Midwest Quarterly, Cottonwood, Briar Cliff Review,* and *A 21st Century Plague: Poetry from a Pandemic.* He lives in St. Paul, Minnesota.

Tim Nolan

Tim Nolan was born in Minneapolis, graduated from the University of Minnesota with a B.A. in English, and from Columbia University in New York City with an M.F.A. in writing. Tim is an attorney in private practice in Minneapolis. His poems have appeared in *The Gettysburg Review, The Nation, The New Republic, Ploughshares,* and on *The Writer's Almanac* and *American Life in Poetry.* His three collections—*The Sound of It, And Then,* and *The Field* have all been published by New Rivers Press.

Dougie Padilla

Dougie Padilla is a life-long minnesota artist/poet/activist/ visionary of norge/mex/cowboy roots and funk/beat/magic-realist/zen/shamanic sensibilities, dougie padilla is a grateful member of the "lucky to be alive" club. he wanders the shores of the ever enchanting mississippi river where, this morning, he enjoyed the icy glare of 52 delightfully surly vultures.

Rebecca Paradis

For over thirty years, Rebecca Paradis has lived on a woodsy lot near the river, where from her second story picture window she observes a fantastic variety of birds flying and feeding.

She is working on a series of poems titled ANOTHER PICTURE WINDOW POEM.

Kate Reilly

By day, Kathryn helps students investigate words' power; at night, she resurrects goddesses and ghosts, spinning new speculative tales. Enjoy poetic adventures in *Shadow Atlas: Dark Landscapes of the Americas, Willow Tree Swing, Last Girls Club, Blink Ink*, and fiction with *Tree and Stone, Seaside Gothic*, and Elly Blue Publishing. She tends a flowering birdseed garden, and can be found rewilding her yard. Twitter: @Katecanwrite

Jim Rogers

James Silas Rogers is an essayist, poet, and editor in St. Paul. He is the author of two poetry collections, and an essay collection Most recently, he edited the anthology *Broad Wings, Long Legs: A Rookery of Heron Poems* (2023).

Northern Orchards: Places Near the Dead (North Star Press of St Cloud, 2014): "The Young Birdwatcher"

Nimrod: "Window Kills," "Crows in Early Winter (Near Black River Falls)"

Emprise Review: "Blackbird in Beloit"

Sundogs (Parallel Press, 2006): "My Grandmother's Childhood"

Carol Rucks

Carol Rucks graduated from the University of Wisconsin, Stevens Point, where she studied Literature and Creative Writing with David Steingass and Dave Engel. She also studied with Jude Nutter and Thomas Smith at the Loft Literary Center, and with Roseann Lloyd in Central American as part of Art Workshops in Guatemala. She has worked mainly in libraries, especially at the Art/Music/Literature reference desk at the Minneapolis Central Library. Her poems have been published in "Abraxas", "West Branch", "Colere", "Earth's Daughters", "Poetry Quarterly", and elsewhere. She is the author of the poetry collection *Evidence of Rain*, published by Nodin Press, and nominated for the Minnesota Book Award. She lives in Minneapolis with her husband Mark McHugh.

Jessica Simmons

Jessica Simmons is a secondary dance teacher in Fort Worth, TX. She explores her creativity through writing, dance, embroidery, and any art form she can get her hands on. Her work has been previously published in *Lamplit Underground*, *Gingerbread House*, and *Miracle Monocle*, among others.

Thomas R. Smith

Thomas R. Smith is a poet and teacher living in River Falls, Wisconsin. Many of his poems are set on the Kinnickinnic River, which runs through the heart of his town. The most recent of his ten poetry collections is *Medicine Year* (Paris Morning Publications, 2022). He is also the author of *Poetry on the Side of Nature: Writing the Nature Poem as an Act of Survival* (Red

Dragonfly Press, 2022). He posts poems and essays at www.
thomasrsmithpoet.com.

Rev. Ted Tollefson

Ted Tollefson is a Unitarian Universalist minister living in the
village of Frontenac, MN with his wife Kristen. He teaches
psychology at Metro State University and for 20 years taught
World Religions at United Theological Seminary. A good day
begins with a cup of tea, a walk in the forest and sometimes a
new poem. His latest collection of poems is called Household
of Joy!

Scott Vetsch

Scott Vetsch has bees in his bonnet, often hearing things
wrong, which sometimes makes them right. He's a carpenter
who works in old houses, a child in a man's body, a soul in exile.
He likes a good story, whichever way it comes, loves cats and
crows, inhabits worlds of his own making. He's afraid things
aren't getting better, but hopes he's mistaken. He burns wood,
craves hamburgers, and eats tofu, scoffs at money, envies the
contented, and drives a truck. When he's happy he wants beer.
When he's sad, he wonders why. He knows one thing for certain,
he's a writer in a post-literate world.

Greg Watson

Greg Watson's work has appeared in numerous literary journals
and anthologies, and has twice been nominated for the Pushcart
Prize. He is the author of nine collections of poetry, most
recently *The Sound of Light*. He is also co-editor with Richard

Broderick of *The Road by Heart: Poems of Fatherhood*, published by Nodin Press.

Timothy Young

Timothy Young's upcoming book, *Threads on the Painting*, will be his fifth book of poetry. Red Dragonfly Press also published, *Portraits of Rodeo Clowns and Royalty* in 2018, *To the Palace of Kings* in 2014, *and Herds of Bears Surround Us* in 2010. His first book, *Building in Deeper Water*, was introduced by Robert Bly and published by the Thousands Press in 2003. His poetry has appeared in Scribner's *The Best American Poetry of 1999* and has been read on *The Writer's Almanac*.

jd hegarty

jd hegarty (she/they) is a poet, an anarchist, and a sunflower living in Minneapolis, Minnesota with two cats. jd's work can be found in Name & None, Crab Orchard Review, Mortar Magazine, 45th Parallel, Inscape and elsewhere. Their first chapbook, On Passing, was published by Red Bird Chapbooks in 2017 and their self-published chapbook of sad gay love poems, the clearest blue, is available for free at jdhegarty.com. They can be found on twitter @YourAuntieJD